NO FAMILY LEFT BEHIND

Jeff Davis

TRILOGY CHRISTIAN PUBLISHERS

Tustin, CA

Trilogy Christian Publishers
A Wholly Owned Subsidiary of Trinity Broadcasting Network
2442 Michelle Drive
Tustin, CA 92780

For information, address Trilogy Christian Publishing

Rights Department, 2442 Michelle Drive, Tustin, Ca 92780.

Trilogy Christian Publishing/ TBN and colophon are trademarks of Trinity Broadcasting Network.

For information about special discounts for bulk purchases, please contact Trilogy Christian Publishing.

Manufactured in the United States of America

10 9 8 7 6 5 4 3 2 1

Library of Congress Cataloging-in-Publication Data is available.

ISBN 978-1-64773-422-0

ISBN 978-1-64773-423-7 (ebook)

Contents

This book is dedicated to the thousands of military families that sacrifice so much in the defense of our great nation. My prayer is that this book offers hope for those who face the highs and lows of a life of service.

A special thanks to my loving wife and friend, Leah.
You have shared this amazing military family
journey and given me something and someone to
fight for. I love you!

ENDORSEMENTS

In this time of great stress and challenge for families, not only military families but the families of all Americans, "No Family Left Behind" is an apt word for such a time as this!

The Biblical principles espoused will be a great help to families as they put these principles into practice. I highly recommend this book!

Commander Jeff Etheridge
Chaplain, US Navy

Jesus came to provide an abundant life for those who would accept Him. This truth is found in the Book of John 10:10 which includes a key word—"I have come that they MIGHT have life, and that they MIGHT have it more abundantly." (KJV) This word reflects the important "choices" we have as we face the battles of life. This book provides practical strategies from God's Word that will strengthen family relationships in the midst of these battles. It has been my privilege to know Captain Jeff Davis for over fourteen years and he is a faithful follower of Christ who models Godly manhood, marriage and fatherhood. He provides powerful insights that will help families navigate the rough terrain and turbulent waters of family relationships. Youwill be blessed as you discover important keys to addressing life's challenges. This is a must read!

Dr. Clifford Ashe

Pastor, Dayspring Ministries
Founder, Mighty Men of Valor

PREFACE

Dear Reader,

It is no secret that families are under increasing pressure in our fast-paced society. The result has been increasing fractures in family relationships that manifest in divorce and growing alienation between family members.

These disturbing trends are magnified in families that face the trauma and stress created by extended absence and dangerous professions. Our nation's military has lived through over eighteen years of continuous war. As a result, these families are on the front lines of a

Global War on Terrorism while also facing internal battles. Like many families, these families face struggles behind closed doors that go unnoticed, chipping away at their foundation.

This book is intended as a rallying cry for these military families and other families who face similar struggles. Important principles drawn from scripture and practical experience provide hope for families in every walk of life. Join me in sounding the rallying cry on behalf of every family so we can ensure that *no family is left behind!*

OPERATION FAMILY RESCUE

I do solemnly swear that I will support and defend the Constitution of the United States against all enemies, foreign and domestic; that I will bear true faith and allegiance to the same; that I take this obligation freely, without any mental reservation or purpose of evasion; and that I will well and faithfully discharge the duties of the office on which I am about to enter. So help me God.

(Military Oath)

This is where it all begins for those who choose a life of military service. This is an individual oath that signals a commitment to fight for something bigger than ourselves. However, this commitment does not remain an individual one. Over time, every military family learns that this oath has a tremendous impact on every member of the family. There are countless fathers, mothers, husbands, wives, sons, daughters, and parents who are all too acquainted with the joys and pains of military service. This book is written as a survival guide for families that struggle with the pressures of military life.

> *This book is written as a survival guide for families that struggle with the pressures of military life.*

INTRODUCTION

After over twenty-seven years of service as a member of the U.S. Armed Forces, I reflect with tremendous pride in the choice that I made those many years ago to serve my nation. Yet that choice has come with tremendous highs and lows that have shaped me over the years as a leader, as a spouse, and as a parent.

Most importantly, these years of service have shaped my family in ways that continue to reverberate. This fact is a source of great satisfaction and at the same time a source of significant regret. You see, like many others before me I understood and valued the importance of concepts like honor, courage, and commitment. These concepts have driven tremendous sacrifice that was borne not only by me but also by my family.

There can be great satisfaction in giving your life to something bigger than yourself rather

> *As military families, we understand the concept of mission so why not harness this important concept and focus on "family" as the mission.*

than the motivations that predominate in lives dedicated to personal gratification. The opportunity to demonstrate this type of sacrifice can be a powerful example within a family unit but it can also be a source of great conflict and resentment that can fester and afflict the military family in ways that are unique and damaging.

This book is intended as a rescue mission for military families that are struggling today, but it is also a campaign plan for the successful execution of what I'd like to call "Operation Family Rescue." The premise of this book is a simple one that I believe will also be useful to military families. As military families, we understand the concept of mission so why not harness this important concept and focus on "family" as the mission.

The source material for this book comes from over twenty-eight years of personal struggles and successes in my own family. It is also derived from my experiences with other military families I have had the opportunity to serve with as a leader, friend and counselor over this same period. This experience has left a profound impression on me.

FAMILY MISSION OBJECTIVE

My prayer is that through this book you will be the beneficiary of the wisdom that comes from evaluated experience—my own experiences and that of dozens of military families I have served with over the years. As a father of four adult children and now a grandfather of three grandsons,

I am convinced that the most effective service I can offer today is to pass along these experiences as transparently as this medium will allow.

FAMILY MISSION ANALYSIS

These experiences will be distilled into key principles that resonate and relate to practical living. I will draw on key examples from the life of a prominent military figure whose life has served as an inspiration to me. History records uniquely transparent details about the personal and professional life of this figure that are available to an extent unlike any other leader. I am referring to none other than King David, who is as well known for his personal indiscretions and failures as he is for his military conquests. His personal family struggles are well documented and provide a great backdrop for dealing with real issues that affect every military family.

As we cover this subject, I will make references to the traditional family unit, but make no mistake, the principles we will cover apply to families of every type. Whether you are a single parent or you face a blended family situation, these principles apply. They apply to the dual military family with both spouses wearing the uniform. It applies to a family that is dealing with infertility and an empty nest just as much as it does to

> ❧
>
> *...every family faces challenges and seasons that can be transformed by applying principles from God's Word.*

the family with a full nest. The one thing that is clear to me after my years of service is that every family faces challenges and seasons that can be transformed by applying principles from God's Word.

The pages that follow contain the content that I would have wanted when beginning my military family journey. Whether you are an E-1 thinking about marriage or have thirty-plus years of experience with children and grandchildren, the message of this book offers hope and counsel with universal applicability. By picking up this book you are acknowledging the most important orders you will ever receive—orders to "Operation Family Rescue."

PRAYER

*Heavenly Father, thank you for my family. Lord, I
desire to walk and live in harmony within my family, just as You desire that we live in unity and love.
There is nothing that can separate us from Your love.
Help me to face and repair the issues that threaten my
family. I commit to applying Your truth to transform
my family relationships because Your blessings and
goodness are found where there is unity.
In Jesus' name, amen.*

SURPRISE ATTACKS

David and his men reached Ziklag on the third day. Now the Amalekites had raided the Negev and Ziklag. They had attacked Ziklag and burned it, and had taken captive the women and everyone else in it, both young and old. They had killed none of them, but carried them off as they went on their way. When David and his men reached Ziklag, they found it destroyed by fire and their wives and sons and daughters taken captive.

1 Samuel 30:1-3 (NIV)

> *...this enemy preys on the fact that your focus and commitment to service and sacrifice will leave your family vulnerable to attack.*

Congratulations! You have taken the first step by accepting your orders to join "Operation Family Rescue." An essential first step is recognizing that there is a reason to fight! There is an enemy that is waging war on your family. There is a terrorist insurgency that cannot be combatted by Homeland Security or the employment of military instruments of power. No Army, Air Force, Navy, or Marine Corps battle plan or tactics can combat this enemy. In fact, this enemy preys on the fact that your focus and commitment to service and sacrifice will leave your family vulnerable to attack.

DEALING WITH SMOKE AND ASH

The Bible passage above illustrates the vulnerability introduced into the family while we serve. In this passage, we find David who is now a young military leader of some renown following his defeat of Goliath. David is now leading soldiers who have chosen to follow and fight by his side even while he is on the run from King Saul. These soldiers had pledged their loyalty to David, who was destined to be the next king, and by doing so they were rejecting King Saul who viewed David as a threat to his illegitimate rule.

A HEART TO SERVE

As we look to the life of David for principles that we can apply in "Operation Family Rescue," it is important to know a little about the character of David at this point in his life. David was the eighth son of Jesse and had spent his youth in the solitary life of a shepherd caring for his father's sheep. This role required David to live apart from his family to fulfill his responsibility to keep constant watch over sheep—helpless animals known for their tendency to wander off. David learned the lessons of faithfulness and responsibility that every leader must learn. Not only was David shaped by the lonely life of a shepherd, he also experienced the painful sting of low expectations.

On one occasion, David's father, Jesse, hosted a reception to allow the prophet Samuel to select one of his sons to be the next king of Israel. David was not even invited to attend this event. In fact, it was only after Samuel had surveyed and rejected all of David's brothers that Jesse called David in from tending sheep. David was such an afterthought that Samuel had to ask Jesse if he had any more sons before Jesse took any steps to call David. In spite of the sting of being initially excluded from the reception, David was anointed to be the next king. Once anointed, David returned to tending sheep and continued to display the heart of a servant.

David's faithfulness was on full display one day as he obeyed his father's request to bring supplies to his brothers who were now serving in the army. David saw his brothers and the rest of the army of Israel cowering at the sight of Goliath and the army of the Philistines. David responded with boldness and faith, defeating Goliath and inspiring the army of Israel to defeat the Philistine enemy.

Just as David's renown increased in Israel, he became the target of King Saul's jealousy. David was pursued by King Saul and his army while living on the run and in caves. Even so, David refused to speak ill of King Saul or to harm him. David was prepared to remain faithful to God and to his men while facing a life in exile through no fault of his own.

Maybe you can relate to David's story of being underestimated, forgotten, or unjustly persecuted. Perhaps that is exactly what led to your passion to serve. Yet that very passion to faithfully serve creates vulnerabilities that we must face if we are going to be successful in "Operation Family Rescue."

SMOKE IN THE DISTANCE

Now, imagine David returning from a military deployment with his soldiers and off in the distance there is a cloud of smoke and ash. Weary from deployment, these warriors are left to face the reality that while they were gone something had transpired that devastated their families. As they surveyed the area, they realized that the lives they thought would be waiting for them were gone!

Can you relate to the depth of the pain and frustration that comes with returning from a mission only to discover that things had changed? I know I can. Even though there was no physical enemy that had come in and burned my possessions and carried away my family, I can recall feeling as though the family I remembered was no longer there. Perhaps it was the smoke of regret for missed ball games and recitals, or the ash of frustration and resentment that my spouse felt for all the tough days she faced alone while I was away and oblivious. In effect, while I was away, my family had been attacked by life.

Sadly, in most cases, we aren't even able to recognize what has occurred and just how profound and devastating these subtle attacks on the family can be.

> *...while I was away, my family had been attacked by life.*

These attacks do not discriminate. Whether you are a single parent returning and attempting to resume your primary caregiver role or you are in a dual military family, the attacks still come. And in some cases these attacks can be even more pronounced.

THE AFTERMATH

In the midst of the smoke and ash, it is easy to focus on what is gone and miss the hope that is evident even in the midst of devastation.

"When David and his men reached Ziklag, they found it destroyed by fire and their wives and sons and daughters taken captive" (1 Samuel 30:3).

Even though they were surrounded by destruction, there was a realization that their most precious possessions, their families, were not destroyed. Their families were captives, but recovery was still possible!

I have seen the heartbreak of service members who return from deployment to find out that their spouse has grown emotionally distant. In some cases, they return to find they have been deserted. Some service members return home to find out their children have begun running with the wrong crowd or are displaying destructive behavior. In the face of desperate family circumstances we can survey the situation and find hope. There was still hope for David and his men because of the realization

> *In the midst of the smoke and ash, it is easy to focus on what is gone and miss the hope that is evident even in the midst of devastation.*

that their families were captives but were not destroyed. Today, I want you to take hope. The message of "Operation Family Rescue" is that recovery is possible!

The harsh reality is that hope is sometimes illusive. In the "real" world it can be hard to see hope in the haze of smoke and ash. David and his men did a very human thing that we all sometimes do. They struggled with the grief over what was gone, even to the point that the Bible records them crying until "they had no strength left to weep" (1 Samuel 30:4). These battle-hardened warriors were so devastated by the tragedy faced at home and in their family that they cried until they had no more tears.

The message of "Operation Family Rescue" is that recovery is possible!

Perhaps you've faced something that hit you so hard you felt completely helpless and ill-equipped to fix the problem. Perhaps it is an out-of-control teen, a spouse who wants to throw in the towel, or the loss of a friend or loved one that placed you in this very human state of helplessness. I have experienced it, and I have seen countless military families walk through this valley of smoke and ash. There is no platitude or catchy phrase that can or should be used to gloss over this type of pain and devastation. That is what I love about the Biblical account of David's life and why he is the perfect example for real people. He faced his grief and pain with an authentically human response that we can relate to and understand.

And just when you thought it couldn't get any worse, David's role as the leader magnifies the pain.

"David was greatly distressed because the men were talking of stoning him; each one was bitter in spirit because of his sons and daughters..." (1 Samuel 30:6).

THE RESPONSE

Here is where David sets an example that we *must* seek to follow. At this lowest point, David is not only grieving his own loss but facing blame and the possibility of literal attack by those he led. It was at this moment in the story that "David encouraged himself in the Lord his God" (1 Samuel 30:6). Instead of continuing to dwell on what was gone, David shifted his attention to what he did have left—a faithful God. He turned to the God who had been faithful to him in the toughest seasons and largest challenges of his life.

David went on to pray for guidance and wisdom about his situation and then he acted upon that guidance. Embracing confidence in God's ability and willingness to help him in his time of trouble, David moved out with his soldiers to recover each of their families. We must follow David's example and seek guidance from the originator of the family—God. God instituted the family.

"The Lord God said, "It is not good for the man to be alone. I will make a helper suitable for him" (Genesis 2:18).

From the beginning of creation God recognized it was "good" for us to operate within a family unit. Whatever your family unit looks like today, one thing is true: there is something good about working within a family unit that cannot be discounted. Even in the midst of the smoke and ash of disappointment and disillu-

> *Instead of continuing to dwell on what was gone, David shifted his attention to what he did have left—a faithful God.*

sionment, we can trust God to provide us the direction that we need to recover and rebuild.

I encourage you to respond to the pain and devastation you face in the same way. David found hope in God and you can too. Scripture reminds us of this truth.

> *Even in the midst of the smoke and ash of disappointment & disillusionment, we can trust God to provide us the direction that we need to recover and rebuild.*

"But without faith it is impossible to please Him; for he who comes to God must believe that He is, and that He is a rewarder of those who diligently seek Him" (Hebrews 11:6).

We must seek Godly counsel and wisdom to face the challenge before us and overcome the pain and devastation that we inevitably face in life and more specifically as military families. In the pages that follow, we will explore the challenges faced by all families and offer practical examples of how we should deal with these tough times. But first we will cover the steps we can take in advance to train for the battle we must face so that no family is left behind.

PRAYER

Heavenly Father, thank You for giving me the courage to fight for my family. I don't know yet what it will look like, but I believe that You have a great plan for us. Help me to look past what is missing and continue to trust You for our future. My desire is to be faithful to you and my family, while faithfully serving my country. Thank You for always remaining faithful to me, never leaving me nor forsaking me. Continue to direct my path so that I may recover and rebuild in seasons of devastation. No matter what changes come my way, I will put my hope and trust in You Lord because I believe You exist and You reward those who diligently seek You.
In Jesus' name, amen.

FAMILY DAMAGE ASSESSMENT

As the ark of the Lord was entering the City of David, Michal daughter of Saul watched from a window. And when she saw King David leaping and dancing before the Lord, she despised him in her heart.

2 Samuel 6:16 (NIV)

Borrowing from the life of David once more, we now find David has ascended to the throne and is now King David, replacing the rejected King Saul who had been killed in battle. In the season of David's greatest triumph, he is able to recover the chest that symbolized God's presence with Israel, the Ark of the Covenant. This was the most sacred possession of the nation of Israel that had been lost by King Saul during a battle years before. The jubilation and excitement surrounding the return of the Ark was so great that David danced with reckless abandon in the presence of his subjects much to the dismay of his wife Michal, King Saul's daughter.

DANCING ALONE

This is a troubling account. Here we see David celebrating one of his greatest achievements, and simultaneously we see his wife disconnected from the event and looking on with disgust. You would think she would be happy for her husband and celebrating with him. So, what gives? To understand this troubling scene, you have to look deeper into the backstory.

You may recall the story of David and Goliath. What you may not remember is that Michal was betrothed to David as a result of his victory over Goliath. Unfortunately, shortly after that betrothal, David had to flee and leave Michal behind because of Saul's intense jealousy and desire to have David killed. David spent years on the run from King Saul and leading his volunteer army to victory after victory, but he was never able to return for Michal.

What we really see here is a spouse who is dealing with the emotions of resentment and a sense of abandonment by the same person that is winning yet another victory. You see, David was extremely successful in executing his mission "out there," but Michal was hurting because she didn't see the same energy being placed on the mission "in here"—the family mission.

Now, when you return to the scene of David's dancing and celebration once more, you can see why she struggles to share in the jubilation and sits in isolation watching from a window. David's success only served to remind her of the abandonment she experienced and still felt deeply. I can imagine Michal thinking, *David has fought and won battles allowing him to return the ark. Why didn't he fight to return me to his side?*

This same troubling scene is played out over and over again in families today. At times it may be the spouse looking out the window at the celebration. At other times it may be a child that feels the neglect and abandonment while peering out that lonely window. Let's explore how this plays out in everyday life and what we can do about it.

ROAD TRIP

On a frost-covered January morning in 1993, my wife Leah and I finished stuffing our remaining belongings into a heavily weighted-down Mitsubishi Galant to begin our military journey. It was our first mission—a road trip from Baton

Rouge, Louisiana to Athens, Georgia to attend our Navy Supply Basic Qualification Course. At the time, Leah was five months pregnant and still dealing with the apprehension that young expecting parents face in their second attempt following a painful miscarriage the year before.

In spite of the apprehension associated with the pregnancy and beginning a new journey together, we began with a hopeful expectation for a future that we would face together. Yep, we had no clue. We had no idea of the kinds of triumphs and trials we would face in the years to come, but that is the wonderful thing about being young and in love. Facing the future with your best friend seems like a great deal, and it is just that until you begin facing the realities of dashed hopes and unfulfilled expectations that inevitably come in life, only more intensely in the military life.

Just as in the case of King David and Michal, the unfilled expectations that occur over time

> ❧
>
> *David was extremely successful in executing his mission "out there," but Michal was hurting because she didn't see the same energy being placed on the mission "in here"—the family mission.*

can create scars and fractures that must be addressed to avoid one family member dancing alone while others remain isolated. We will review how this type of scene plays out in families and how to avoid repeating the alienation and isolation that existed between David and Michal.

PRAYER

Heavenly Father, thank You for giving me an opportunity to fight for my family. I repent for falling away from the loving actions that I performed at the start of my relationships. Help me to love as You love, displaying patience and kindness and avoiding envy, boasting, and arrogance. I choose today to grow in love that will forgive faults rather than seek to find faults. I trust You to give me strength as I commit to be an encourager that forgives so that no member of my family will ever have to dance alone.
In Jesus' name, amen.

CONFRONTING VULNERABILITIES

A primary challenge of military life is the task of balancing the expectations and requirements of military life with fulfilling responsibilities as a spouse and later as a parent.

The first clash of expectations was dealing with how to get support from my new military overseers to attend high risk pregnancy medical appointments and classes considering many of these Battalion and Company leaders had no children and no clue why they should support such a request. Because of my unique circumstance, my young mind struggled with whether I should even ask for such an allowance. I would love to write here that I passed the test and ideally balanced my responsibility to my new career and my young and vulnerable spouse but that is not my story. I struggled with this and hesitated to ask for permission to be there for my spouse out of a desire to not be seen as a problem or needy sailor.

> *My actions reflected a willingness to sacrifice support for my spouse to project invulnerability and self-sufficiency.*

My actions reflected a willingness to sacrifice support for my spouse to project invulnerability and self-sufficiency. Maybe you have never made such a poor trade-off as the one I made at this point in my life. If so, great—

that is one less crack in your family relationship foundation. Sadly, I believe my approach is not uncommon based on the "service" and "commitment" mindset that is part of the fabric of the military life.

I have seen my son-in-law, who is a young soldier, face the same challenges as he attempts to balance his responsibility as a soldier with his commitment as a husband and father of two young toddlers. In the twenty-six-year span between my first experience with this phenomenon and what I see my son-in-law balance, it is clear to me that this is a fundamental challenge that every family must face. How these situations are handled has significant implications, leaving imprints on the family shaping priorities and future expectations. These imprints can bring families together or introduce fractures that deepen over time.

Over the next few months leading up to the birth of our daughter, I was able to do better seeking and gaining opportunities to be there for prenatal appointments and classes. Again, I wish I could say that this was a slam dunk but that is not how relationships and families work. A seed was already planted. That seed communicated that family obligations would compete unfavorably with military commitments unless the family need was sufficiently critical.

Even now as I write this as a father of four adult children and as a grandfather, I believe this seed still impacts their expectations of me as a spouse, parent, and grandfather. For years I found myself asking them, "Why didn't you ask me? I could have taken care of that." Only to get the response, "We didn't want to bother you with it."

This is an extraordinary testament of the strength and resilience of the military family but at the same time is extremely painful to me. I somehow created an environment where my family did not want to bother me because something else was more important to me than they were. As I rehearse in my mind the years of being preoccupied with the mission "out there" I now know that I failed to signal the importance of the mission "in here"—I failed to communicate that family was the most important mission.

SEEDS AND WEEDS

This simple example of how expectations can be shaped over time to create cracks in the foundation of the family is important. Over the course of nearly twenty-nine years of marriage and serving in the military for twenty-seven of those years, I have learned a few things. It just so happens that I've learned a little about lawn maintenance. Quick disclaimer, I know more about lawn maintenance than I have successfully executed. It just so happens, that actually helps me tell this story.

We have moved over fourteen times in the past twenty-seven years and in those moves I often find myself trying to nurse a neglected lawn back to health. Sometimes the neglect predated my arrival, and sometimes the neglect occurred during my occupancy. What I have learned is that when weeds (bad seeds) take root, they are not detectable until the spring when everything starts to grow. At that point, what you thought was a fairly healthy but dormant lawn begins to show the clear signs that the lawn has been invaded and compromised by weeds.

At this point, there are two choices. You can take the extreme step of pulling up the lawn and replanting the lawn. The other option is to manage the damage with weed suppressants, then re-seed, fertilize, and treat the lawn in the fall. Okay, since this is not a lawn care book you might ask, *where is he going with this story?* I have learned that the principles that govern nature also apply to our family relationships.

Over time, weeds are planted in our relation-ships. I provided you a good example of one type—the low expectation/priority weed. Once plant-ed, this weed is often dor-mant until the spring rainy seasons of life appear. You know the times I'm talk-ing about. These are times when things appear to be going just fine but all of a sudden you begin seeing signs of prickly behav-ior. This behavior manifests in the form of com-ments like, "you always...." or "you never..." or even "I knew you would be too busy."

> *Over time, weeds are planted in our relationships.*

DEALING WITH THE WEEDS

"As long as the earth endures, seed time and harvest, cold and heat, summer and winter, day and night will never cease."

Genesis 8:22 (NIV)

In these seasons we must understand that we have to respond to these weeds in the same way nature dictates. Applying the lessons of seeds and weeds provides a helpful guide to recovering healthy family relationships in the wake of issues caused by life. Just as scripture reminds us that "seedtime and harvest" will never cease, there are established principles that we can apply to cultivate strong families. These principles can be summarized in four steps.

Step One: Recognizing the Weeds

Every family must face the reality that weeds are present. Just as in nature, weeds are a naturally occurring phenomenon in family relationships. Years ago, my wife and I attended a marriage seminar at a church and the facilitators began by telling us about how they never fight. After over twenty-eight years of marriage, I can tell you that if you meet a marriage counselor that tells you they are in a relationship free of conflict—run! In the real world, there will always be differences

Every family must face the reality that weeds are present. Just as in nature, weeds are a naturally occurring phenomenon in family relationships.

that must be addressed and because it is the real world, we will not always address those differences well. As a result, there will be opportunities for weeds to grow.

Recognizing that it is extremely likely there are weeds lying dormant waiting to spring up will help you to remain vigilant in your relationships and avoid the neglect that allows weeds to grow. Ignoring weeds will produce disastrous results in your family. Recognizing the presence of weeds is the first step to arresting the effects of weeds that will otherwise take over and destroy your family relationships.

Step Two: Treating the Weeds

Another important lesson my years of lawn maintenance have taught me is the importance of treating for weeds. In years past, I spent more time than I want to admit pulling weeds from my lawn. Over time, I noticed a disturbing trend.

I ended up with these patches of dirt that were reminders of weeds that once occupied the soil. It was an exhausting battle as I pulled up weeds each day only to have new ones spring up a few days later.

I then learned of a great product called "Weed & Feed" that was safe for my lawn but worked to stifle the growth of the weeds. This miracle formula saved my back and helped me to maintain a healthier lawn. But even with this new miracle formula I found out that I needed to be deliberate and disciplined about applying these lawn treatments consistently and at the right time of season to get the best results.

This lesson also applies to our family relationships. There are seasons when the application of treatments like acts of kindness, displays of affection, and acts of service will produce greater results. We have to remain alert for "special" occasions and stay vigilant in doing the routine things like speaking words of affirmation that

> *There are seasons when the application of treatments like acts of kindness, displays of affection, and acts of service will produce greater results.*

will keep weeds at bay in your relationships. Look for opportunities to apply patience and compassion while also identifying and removing your actions that contribute to weeds in your relationships.

Step Three: Re-Planting Good Seed

Now that you have taken treatment steps and removed damaging behaviors of neglect, rejection, and bitterness, you are now positioned to contribute new healthy seed. Re-planting is done by exhibiting healthy behaviors and making wise choices. These choices include being intentional about reconnecting without being dismissive about what other family members have faced or are currently facing. Our choices also include avoiding assumptions about what should be acceptable in the relationship.

> *Re-planting is done by exhibiting healthy behaviors and making wise chocies.*

We must be prepared to establish new boundaries as needed to accommodate the changes and growth that has occurred while you have been apart. Here, our objective is to plant healthy seed that is well suited to the environment. In some cases, quality time will be the right seed; in other cases, acts of service may be the appropriate seed to apply. We must remain attentive and receptive to the moments and seasons to apply the new seed.

Step Four: Fertilize the New Seed

> *The time for fertilizing is whenever the opportunity to do so is presented. What I have learned is that these times don't always occur on the schedule and in the moments we would choose.*

Fertilizing the new seed implies a commitment to sustaining the growth of the healthy relationships we all desire. The time for fertilizing is whenever the opportunity to do so is presented. What I have learned is that these times don't always occur on the schedule and in the moments we would choose. This makes it all the more important that we are paying attention to the seasons and moments that arise so we can affirm one another and reinforce the importance of family relationships. Be prepared to put in the time and consistency required. This is an investment that you will never regret.

APPLYING THE TREATMENT

There is a deeper truth in the prescription above. Every family has to deal with weeds. If you are tempted to think, this is good advice for that struggling family I know, think again. Remember, the first step is recognizing the weeds are there—even if they are dormant and not visible, you will still benefit from taking time to survey

... you will still benefit from taking time to survey your relationships and ask yourself some hard questions.

your relationships and ask yourself some hard questions:

- *Am I prioritizing the relationships in my life appropriately?*
- *How would my family answer that question?*
- *Does my family believe they are my Priority Mission?*
- *Are my decisions and actions demonstrating my family is my Priority Mission?*

Answering these questions will help you to move to mission execution phases of Treating, Re-planting, and Fertilizing. Ultimately, it always comes down to execution. Successful execution of "Operation Family Rescue" requires action. Now, let's get started!

PRAYER

Heavenly Father, thank you for revealing the existence of weeds in my relationships. You have not given us a spirit of fear, but of power and love and self-control. Give me wisdom and grace to apply patience and speak words of affirmation that will encourage and strengthen my family. I will plant Your Word in my heart so I can turn away from attitudes and mindsets that erode my relationships and hurt those who I love. Help me to renew my mind so that I see things from Your perspective. Thank you for giving me grace for the journey as I commit to making the family mission my priority mission.

In Jesus' name, amen.

WHO IS ON WATCH?

For twenty years
This sailor has stood the watch
While some of us were in our bunks at night
This sailor stood the watch
While some of us were in school learning our trade
This shipmate stood the watch
Yes, even before some of us were born into this world
This shipmate stood the watch
In those years when the storm clouds of war were seen
*   brewing on the horizon of history*
This shipmate stood the watch

Many times he would cast an eye ashore and see his
   family standing there
Needing his guidance and help
Needing that hand to hold during those hard times
But he still stood the watch

He stood the watch for twenty years
He stood the watch so that we, our families and
Our fellow countrymen could sleep soundly in safety,
   Each and every night
Knowing that a sailor stood the watch
Today we are here to say
"Shipmate... the watch stands relieved
Relieved by those you have rained, Guided, and Led
Shipmate you stand relieved... we have the watch..."
                                            (The Watch)

An important first step in "Operation Family Rescue" is recognizing the unique circumstances faced by military families. We have already mentioned the difficulties created by long periods of separation and the added stress generated by deployments to combat zones or performing duties with inherent danger. When separation becomes the norm, developing and maintaining healthy family relationships becomes infinitely harder.

One of the strongest traditions of the US Navy is the concept of standing "The Watch," described in the quoted text above. This concept captures the nature of service that relies on the discipline and faithfulness of the individual to ensure the success of the team. One of the first things every sailor learns is the importance of standing the watch, which signifies you are qualified and

> *This concept captures the nature of service that relies on the discipline and faithfulness of the individual to ensure the success of the team.*

trusted to contribute to the team in a significant way. A sailor's eligibility to stand the watch is usually preceded by study and testing to ensure the sailor possesses the requisite knowledge and discipline to be trusted. A life of service is underscored by commitment, discipline, and sacrifice that is epitomized by "The Watch."

A LIFE OF SERVICE

If there is one thing military families understand it's that service comes at a price. Sustaining healthy relationships becomes a daunting task when the mission "out there" conflicts with the mission "in here" (at home). I've read wonderful family and marriage books that begin with emphasizing the importance of demonstrating the priority of these family relationships in tangible ways. Unfortunately, these books tend to be light on examples of fathers and mothers who have to explain to their children why they remain in professions that require them to be separated from them for months on end in inherently dangerous environments. These families grapple with the ideal of submitting to a call that requires great sacrifice by those who have taken oaths of service and understand concepts like duty and sacrifice in ways that many can't. This point is powerfully expressed in "The Watch":

> *Sustaining healthy relationships becomes a daunting task when the mission "out there" conflicts with the mission "in here" (at home).*

"Many times he would cast an eye ashore and see his family standing there
Needing his guidance and help

Needing that hand to hold during those hard times
But he still stood the watch."

(The Watch)

⬗⬗⬗

This life of service requires recognizing that sacred oaths often impact family members who never had an opportunity to choose and who made no oaths and are sometimes too young to understand them.

This life of service requires recognizing that sacred oaths often impact family members who never had an opportunity to choose and who made no oaths and are sometimes too young to understand them.

I can recall my third major deployment that occurred when my twin sons were two-year-olds and my two daughters were five- and seven-year-olds. On a dark night pulling onto the base, we drove slowly to the parking area a few hundred yards from the aircraft carrier I would be deploying on for the next seven months. As I began to park, I remember the dreaded question: "Why do you have to go, Daddy?" At that moment I struggled to respond in a way that could help to explain the apparent contradiction of a parent seemingly choosing to leave a family that I loved dearly. I began with, "You know Daddy loves you very much." I continued by saying, "There are mommies and daddies who have to go away to ensure they keep all of us safe. They have taken their turn keeping us all safe, and now it is Daddy's turn to go so they can come home to their families now."

Of course, they still didn't want to see Daddy go. However, I believe this was a baptism in the principle of serving a cause greater than self that will always be a part of how they see the world.

A LIFE APART

Here again, I wish I could say that the simple heartfelt message I shared with my family on that dark night on the pier greatly eased the pain and challenges that are part of long deployments. But those who have experienced it and those who are currently experiencing the pain of separation know better. Words cannot erase the angst and concern that families have for their deployed loved one any more than it can ease the guilt and frustration of the deployed family member who wishes they could be there for those important moments for their families.

Most service members have learned how to throw themselves into the mission "out there" and remain focused in ways that allow the long days to be bearable. Unfortunately, there are long days at home that must be navigated by military families trying to keep up with all the emotional, physical, and financial demands on the family. During this time, the family members often discover reservoirs of strength that can only be found in times of immense pressure and stretching.

A spouse or family member that has developed their own coping mechanisms for handling daily responsibilities may struggle with reverting to old ways. What these families may overlook is that the

> *What these families may overlook is that the reservoir of strength developed during their season apart can also create a moat that must be crossed when the deployed family member returns and attempts to assume their former roles in the home.*

reservoir of strength developed during their season apart can also create a moat that must be crossed when the deployed family member returns and attempts to assume their former roles in the home.

THE RETURN

Failure to recognize the changes that have occurred during this period of separation creates expectation mismatch and in some cases resentment. As a result, the returning family member looks out at the moat that was constructed in their absence shouting for their families to lower the draw bridge and is

> *Failure to recognize the changes that have occurred during this period of separation creates expectation mismatch and in some cases resentment.*

shocked to hear a familiar voice on the other side of the moat shouting, "Swim!"

Let me be clear here when I say that this phenomenon is a common one and should not be viewed from the perspective of right or wrong behavior. When you are dealing with human behavior and response to what constitutes a traumatic experience of separation and loss, you have to understand this as a "natural" phenomenon.

It signals the need to adjust expectations and grow into new roles. In some cases, we can assume old responsibilities and in other cases we must prepare to share these responsibilities and take on new ones. There is no one size fits all, but the common theme is that family members must recognize that change has *already* occurred and they have to be prepared to face that change and adjust their roles and expectations accordingly.

A danger in any relationship is the tendency for one person to take a snapshot in time and forever respond to their friend, spouse or child

> ❧
>
> *A danger in any relationship is the tendency for one person to take a snapshot in time and forever respond to their friend, spouse or child based on that snapshot.*

based on that snapshot. We have all seen it before. We can quickly spot the inappropriateness of parents who treat their adult children like kids. We can also spot the awkwardness of trying to relate to old friends you have not seen since grade school only to come to the conclusion that neither of you are the same person. Those old assumptions are just not very useful and must be cast aside as you learn to relate with the person that stands before you today.

This is exactly what we must be prepared to do with our families as we reacclimate following lengthy separations. Here again the most important thing is to recognize the need to begin this process of relearning. There is no simple pat answer that I can offer other than to encourage you to resist the temptation to mourn what is past. We must focus our attention on the new mission, rebuilding trust and paying attention to assume new roles as opportunities are presented. It's important to note that this is not a license for passivity.

You recall the voice from the other side of the moat that said "Swim!" That is exactly what you must be prepared to do. Take action to reconnect and gain entrance but do so with awareness that the operator of the draw bridge is also operating the gates of the castle. We must be prepared to swim by listening for the opportunities for greater connection and seeking to grow together as a family. This means being able to compromise and pivot from "my way" and "your way" to develop a new "our way".

We must be prepared to swim by listening for the opportunities for greater connection and seeking to grow together as a family.

Listen for signs that you are applying old assumptions to relate to a person who has changed. Your spouse, your children, and you for that matter, will grow and change over time. You will need to make room for that growth and change as you seek to regain access to the castle.

PRAYER

Father, Your love for me is perfectly demonstrated by the willing sacrifice of Your Son for mankind. This was the greatest act of service. Give me wisdom and strength to prioritize my family as we experience separation and change. Help me to humbly balance the changes and growth that naturally occur in times of separation in order to strengthen my family. Let me always remember the importance of honor and respect inside the home as much as I do outside of the home. Help me to cherish and value the family that I have without fixating on the past or the ideal. Give me the courage to forgive and the humility to seek forgiveness when there are wounds in my family relationships. Help me to commit myself to learning how to serve in the home with a greater passion and intensity even as I learn to serve You with sincerity and faith.

In Jesus' name, amen.

INSIDER THREATS

In the spring, at the time when kings go off to war, David sent Joab out with the king's men and the whole Israelite army. They destroyed the Ammonites and besieged Rabbah. But David remained in Jerusalem.

2 Samuel 11:1 (NIV)

In this nondescript opening text of chapter 11 of the book of 2 Samuel there is a brief sentence that had a seismic impact on King David's life. The verse begins by declaring it was a season "when kings go off to war," then ends with what appears to be an innocent statement of fact.

"But David remained in Jerusalem" (2 Samuel 11:1 NIV).

RELAXED DEFENSES

In the last chapter we highlighted the cost that is paid by families who serve and the challenges that are faced as we work desperately to balance the mission "out there" with the mission "in here" (the family). In section two of this book, we recounted the story of David and his band of warriors returning from victory "out there" to smoke and ash. This was a powerful picture of the devastation that can sometimes occur when our focus is on the mission out there.

In the verse above, we see that King David has his army dispatched winning victories but he is actually at home. He is physically present but as we shall see, he faces the most devastating attack on his family while being at home. This was an attack that would fragment his family and his descendants for generations. Again, there is much we can learn from David's life that reflects the human condition as well as any documented life in human history. David was a celebrated leader, general, and king and yet he made mistakes that devastated his family and provides an excellent illustration for us all.

The remainder of 2 Samuel chapter 11, presents a sordid tale of Kind David in a moment of leisure peering out his window and observing a beautiful woman named Bathsheba bathing. Infatuated by her beauty he sends for her knowing that her husband

> *David was a celebrated leader, general, and king and yet he made mistakes that devastated his family and provides an excellent illustration for us all.*

was away fighting in the Israelite army—King David's army. The outcome was an affair that left Bathsheba pregnant and David manufacturing a suicide mission for her husband Uriah to ensure the affair would not be discovered. David's actions led to a cascade of negative consequences ranging from the death of the child conceived in the affair to the betrayal and temporary overthrow of his thrown by Absalom, the son he loved.

It would not be difficult to point to the importance of integrity and faithfulness in fostering positive relationships. David violated both of these key principles, and when principles are violated there are always consequences regardless of your position and title. In recent years, we have seen a carousel of senior leaders with indiscretions that have destroyed their families and reputations making their stories cautionary tales.

The message should be clear but I believe it is overly simplistic to focus on David's obvious indiscretions and overlook the greater issue and lesson to be gleaned. David's story demonstrates that being present is not enough! We must be deliberate about protecting the family and executing the mission "in here" or we will be vulnerable to making or allowing decisions to be made that are destructive to the family. An often overlooked truth about the Garden of Eden is that Eve was not alone when she de-

> *David's story demonstrates that being present is not enough! We must be deliberate about protecting the family and executing the mission "in here" or we will be vulnerable to making or allowing decisions to be made that are destructive to the family.*

cided to eat the forbidden fruit. Adam was right beside her because in Genesis 3:6 it is recorded that after she ate she turned and gave the fruit to Adam and he ate. Just as in the case of David, Adam was present yet his presence did not reflect a focus on protecting the first family.

Making the family your Priority Mission means ensuring you remain engaged. Continue listening and seeking to provide what is needed to preserve unity and trust. Continue seeking to encourage and develop one another in ways that will result in lasting healthy family relationships and personal fulfillment for each member of the family.

LINGERING SCARS: FAMILIES IN CRISIS

Our nation has been at war for over eighteen years and the impacts on the family are substantial. We have countless families impacted by the scars of war and deep wounds that cannot be seen or touched with medical instrumentation. Our military families are left to grapple with reestablishing bonds fractured by physical, mental, and emotional trauma.

The trauma that begins in the service member reverberates throughout the family as the spouse, children, parents, friends, and caregivers are left struggling to pick up the pieces. In some cases there is physical impairment or traumatic brain injury created by an improvised explosive device that creates

> *The trauma that begins in the service member reverberates throughout the family as the spouse, children, parents, friends, and caregivers are left struggling to pick up the pieces.*

a new normal that is defined by endless medical rehabilitation. In other cases there are deep scars that affect the personality and rob sleep, creating instability and even fear in the home. And in other cases there may be hidden wounds that remain invisible until surfacing as suicidal ideation and an epidemic of suicide. Sadly, nearly twenty veterans commit suicide each day.

These are issues that deserve far more coverage than I am qualified to provide. However, I realize the pain and desperation created by these situations are unquestionably part of the fabric of the military family. I have included references to resources available to families who face these struggles in section eight of this book. My message to you is that you are not alone. There is a greater military family that has not forgotten your struggle. We are praying for you, and resources are available to help you weather this difficult season. Most importantly, you can place confidence in a God that cares for you, especially in times of crisis.

In chapter six of the Book of Judges, we find the Bible character Gideon cowering with the rest of the nation of Israel in a time when they are surrounded by marauding enemies. Gideon is attempting to thresh wheat in a wine press in hopes of concealing this harvest from enemies who had a practice of coming in and destroying Israel's harvest to keep them poor and weak. When the angel of the Lord appears to Gideon saying, "The Lord is with you,

There is a greater military family that has not forgotten your struggle. We are praying for you, and resources are available to help you weather this difficult season.

> ❧
>
> *Our ability to trust that "the Lord is with us" rests on our faith in His character as expressed in scripture and reflecting on how He has helped us to overcome crisis in the past.*

mighty warrior" (Judges 6:12), Gideon certainly did not appear to fit the label. We see Gideon then asking a pivotal question:

"Pardon me, my Lord," Gideon replied, "but if the Lord is with us, why has all this happened to us? Where are all his wonders that our ancestors told us about when they said, 'Did not the Lord bring us up out of Egypt?' But now the Lord has abandoned us and given us into the hand of Midian."

Judges 6:13 (NIV)

Our ability to trust that "the Lord is with us" rests

on our faith in His character as expressed in scripture and reflecting on how He has helped us to overcome crisis in the past.

God understands our questions and does not condemn us for seeking answers. Our loving Father is not threatened by questions about His nature and intent for His children. In fact, our God has established an excellent track record of listening to the cries of His children. He did so when He called Moses to deliver Israel from the bondage of Egypt.

The Lord said, "I have indeed seen the misery of my people in Egypt. I have heard them crying out because of their slave drivers, and I am concerned about their suffering."

Exodus 3:7 (NIV)

God wants to answer our questions in times of crisis once and for all, but He will continue to answer them as many times as required in our

> *God hears our cry in times of crisis and has a plan for deliverance that will bring us through crisis into a new season.*

lives. Here is what God wants you to understand in the midst of your crisis. God hears our cry in times of crisis and has a plan for deliverance that will bring us through crisis into a new season. Today, let God settle it in your heart. He sees you! He is concerned about your suffering in times of crisis, and our Savior experienced and understands suffering like no other. We can trust Him in our crisis!

PRAYER

*Heavenly Father, thank You for being my rock, my
fortress, and my deliverer in the darkest times. Help
me to keep guard and remain vigilant on my mission
in the home. You offer a place of refuge when my heart
is weary and I struggle with fear and depression. I
look to You for salvation and deliverance. You are the
God who is able to bind up the brokenhearted. You
proclaim freedom when I struggle to find hope. You
trade Your beauty for the ashes of my past. Help me
to overcome doubt by meditating on Your faithfulness even in desperate times. I place my confidence in
You because I know that You waste no pain. Give me
courage to deal transparently and seek help with the
hidden wounds that afflict me so that I can be healed
and bring healing to others. I submit my life fully
to You and embrace the hope that comes from Your
example of love.
In Jesus' name, amen.*

MAKING IT COUNT

David said, "My son Solomon is young and inexperienced, and the house to be built for the Lord should be of great magnificence and fame and splendor in the sight of all the nations. Therefore I will make preparations for it." So David made extensive preparations before his death.

1 Chronicles 22:5 (NIV)

"Operation Family Rescue" requires a generational commitment. Our nation has long been defended by those who had members of their

> *"Operation Family Rescue" requires a generational commitment.*

families serve before them. Less than 1 percent (Reynolds and Shendruk 2018) of the population serves (or has served) in our armed forces. Keeping our nation strong necessitates that we work to keep our military families strong. This is a generational issue, and we must both recognize it and be prepared to step up to the challenge of healing our families today and for the generations to come.

In the verses above, David recognizes the limitations and needs of his son Solomon. He chooses to make sacrifices, gathering resources that Solomon would need to complete a family mission that he had received from God—the construction of a great temple.

The Bible records that David collected construction material and precious metals that would likely be valued in the billions of dollars by today's standards to enable this project to be completed after his death. Like most of us, David faced both victories and defeats over the course of his life. However, through his experiences he developed awareness that there was a mission objective that would outlive him. David clearly learned from his most painful experiences and developed a perspective that allowed him to balance the needs of his family, and by addressing those needs, he allowed a generational family mission to be achieved. David grew from a young man with a "vision" for his future into an older man with a "dream" for his family and descendants. The prophet Joel said it this way:

"And afterward, I will pour out my Spirit on all people. Your sons and daughters will prophesy, your old men will dream dreams, your young men will see visions" (Joel 2:28).

In this context, vision represents something that can be accomplished in your lifetime and dreams represent something that is bigger than you and extends beyond your lifetime. We should all grab hold of the power of having a dream for our families that can transcend our own capacity and ability. David had come to grips with his mortality and was inspired to help his son complete what had become a family dream.

David also understood both the power and the limitations

> *David also understood both the power and the limitations presented by the youth of his son Solomon and made preparations to ensure he gave Solomon the best opportunity to be successful.*

presented by the youth of his son Solomon and made preparations to ensure he gave Solomon the best opportunity to be successful. He did this in three important ways:

1. He transferred a *vision* to Solomon of the importance of the family mission.
2. He provided *resources* to give Solomon a head start at achieving the family mission
3. He imparted *wisdom* to Solomon based on his evaluated experience that had taught him so much over the years.

TRANSFERRING VISION

Every mission is guided by a vision for the future. Just as in the mission "out there" we must ensure that our families have a vision that helps us to make sense of the mission "in here." For my family the vision is the development of men and women of faith and character that will posi-

> *Every mission is guided by a vision for the future.*

tively influence their communities and world. Our mission is to build a family that lives with confidence and courage centered on an awareness of God's faithfulness.

Each member of my family must determine how to focus this courage and confidence to achieve the vision of "positively influencing their communities and world." This is a process of discovery for each of us that add to the richness of each of our lives. I marvel at the paths I see my adult children taking as they discover their unique God-given purpose. It is clear to me today that the experiences we shared—especially the painful ones—have created a richness in each of our lives that has been incredibly rewarding. I watch with wonder as I see them display courage, discipline, and integrity in the face of life's challenges that reflects the lessons they learned in a life of service.

PREPARING RESOURCES

Every family is different but every family has resources that can be shared to support the mission. In my family it was the encouragement to pursue opportunities. My parents grew up in Louisiana as children of sharecroppers and had very limited educational opportunity. Yet, they encouraged me to pursue educational opportunity. As a brick mason, my father taught me the importance of hard work and consistency as he remained faithful to pro-

> *Every family is different but every family has resources that can be shared to support the mission.*

viding for his wife and nine children. He continues to teach me as he and my mother celebrate over sixty-four years of marriage.

For some families, the resource provided is important experiences gained from activities that develop talents and character (e.g. Scouts, Awana, sports, music, etc.). And yes, for some it is financial provision to pursue goals. The key here is that your family has resources to pass along.

Making family a Priority Mission means you will also make it a key priority to pass along resources that will result in generational mission success. I recall reading the pledges made by both Warren Buffet and Bill Gates that they would not leave their vast fortunes to their children. Warren Buffet declared, "You should leave your children enough so they can do anything, but not enough so they can do nothing." (Au-Yeung 2018). Reportedly, Buffet intends on leaving his children each "only" $2 billion of his over $38 billion fortune.

I suspect you are not struggling with how many billions you should leave as an inheritance. Yet, I do believe there is an important principle here that we can all apply. As you look to the next generation, here is a wise standard to apply:

Be intentional about passing along to the next generation enough to pursue their dreams but not so much that they have no reason to dream.

IMPARTING WISDOM

The final and most important thing that David passed along to his son, Solomon, was wisdom from his experience and also from his mistakes. In fact, Solomon was ultimately described as the wisest man that ever lived. He is known for recording the Book of Proverbs also known as the Book of Wisdom. Throughout this book, Solomon speaks of the importance of gaining wisdom and recounts the words of wisdom he received from his father.

> *...a family mission is inherently a generational mission that requires the transferrence of wisdom and knowledge.*

Likewise, a family mission is inherently a generational mission that requires the transference of wisdom and knowledge. We must ensure we are taking the time to allow this transference to take place.

FINAL THOUGHTS

The contributions of the military family to our nation are immense and too often these same families struggle in silence. Invisible chains of isolation, loneliness, and grief predominate and must be addressed honestly to ensure No Family is Left Behind.

Perhaps you are dealing with traumatic injury, illness, marital challenges, financial issues, or the loss of a loved one. My message to you is to reach out for help. There are tremendous resources available to military families. I have included in section eight of this book a list of the many resources available to military families for your reference. Don't suffer in silence. This Sailor still has *The Watch*, and I want to see you get the resources that you need to succeed so that *no family is left behind!*

PRAYER

Father, open the eyes of my heart to see the wonderful plan that You have for my family. Let me see hope in moments of desperation. Help me to live with an awareness of the eternal hope that You offer through the sacrifice of Your Son, as my trust and confidence is placed in You. Today, I commit myself to the Family Mission that is both generational and eternal. Help me to encourage and prepare those You have placed in my life to accomplish our shared mission while embracing the vision that You provide through Your Word. Help me to live a life that honors You and blesses the world around me as I serve. Because I believe in You and place my trust and hope in You, I have confidence You will never leave me. I know my family will never be left behind because You have us in Your hands.

In Jesus' name, amen.

FAMILY RESOURCES

Listed in alphabetical order

DEPLOYMENT

https://www.military.com/deployment
https://www.militaryonesource.mil
https://www.militaryspouse.com
http://www.operationwearehere.com/index.
   html

EDUCATION

https://armedservicesministry.org
https://bluestarfam.org
https://efmpeducationdirectory.militaryone-
    source.mil
https://www.militaryspouse.com
https://www.militaryonesource.mil
https://www.va.gov

FAMILY AND FINANCIAL

https://bluestarfam.org
https://militaryfamilies.com
https://www.militaryfamily.org
https://www.militaryonesource.mil

MENTAL HEALTH

https://www.health.mil
https://www.militaryonesource.mil/
　　health-wellness
https://suicidepreventionlifeline.org
https://www.tricare.mil
https://www.va.gov
https://www.veteranscrisisline.net/get-help/
　　military-crisis-line

SPIRITUAL

https://www.bible.com
https://www.biblegateway.com
https://www.biblestudytools.com

BIBLIOGRAPHY

Au-Yeung, Angel. "Warren Buffett's Advice On
How To Raise Well-Adjusted Heirs." Forbes,
1 June 2018, https://www.forbes.com/sites/
angelauyeung/2018/06/01/warren-buffetts-
advice-on-how-to-raise-well-adjusted-
heirs/#6e9b71af712f.

Elkins, Kathleen. "Billionaires Warren Buffett
and Bill Gates Have Similar Ideas about How
Much Money You Should Leave Your Kids."
CNBC, 26 Sept. 2016, https://www.cnbc.
com/2016/09/26/warren-buffett-bill-gates-

have-similar-ideas-on-how-much-money-to-
leave-kids.html.

Reynolds, George M, and Amanda Shendruk.
"Demographics of the U.S. Military." Council
on Foreign Relations, Council on Foreign
Relations, 24 Apr. 2018, www.cfr.org/article/
demographics-us-military.

The Bible. New International Version. YouVer-
sion, LifeChurch, 2008

"The Watch." The Watch, www.goatlocker.org/
retire/watch.htm.